Freedom or Security?

JUDITH ANDERSON

W
FRANKLIN WATTS
LONDON•SYDNEY

First published in 2006 by Franklin Watts
338 Euston Road, London NW1 3BH

Franklin Watts Australia
Hachette Children's Books
Level 17/207 Kent Street
Sydney NSW 2000

Copyright © Franklin Watts 2006

Editor: Adrian Cole
Series design: White Design
Picture research: Diana Morris

A CIP catalogue record for this book is available from the British Library.

ISBN-10: 0-7496-6930-6
ISBN-13: 978-0-7496-6930-0

Dewey Classification: 323.44'82

Printed in China

Acknowledgements:

Shakil Adil/AP/Empics: 19. AP/Empics: 5t, 7b, 23b, 28l. Oded Balilty/AP/Empics: 26.
Ed Bentz/AP/Empics: 29. Bettmann/Corbis: 6b. Ashwini Bhata/AP/Empics: 21. Cardinael/Rex
Features: 15b. Dan Charity/Rex Features: 16b. Mary Evans Picture Library: 6t. David R. Frazier/
Image Works/Topfoto: 24. Ng Han Guan/AP/Empics: 20. David Guttenfelder/AP/Empics: 28c.
Achmad Ibrahim/AP/Empics: 12. Peter De Jong/AP/Empics: 8. Shane T. McCoy/AP/Empics: 13.
PA/Empics: 5b, 16t, 22c, 27. John Powell/Rex Features: 11. Stephan Rousseau/PA/Empics: 14.
Ali al-Saad/AP/Empics: 4. Alex Segre/Rex Features: 17t. Marc Serota/Reuters/Corbis: 18.
Sipa Press/Rex Features: 10, 15t, 22-23t, 25. David Sproule/Newspix: 9.
Kirsty Wigglesworth/PA/Empics: front cover.

Every attempt has been made to clear copyright. Should there be any
inadvertent omission please apply to the publisher for rectification.

Franklin Watts is a division of Hachette Children's Books.

CONTENTS

WHOSE RIGHTS?

'EVERYONE HAS THE RIGHT TO LIFE, *liberty and security of person.' So says the Declaration of Human Rights, adopted by the United Nations (UN) in 1948 as a standard for all countries of the world (see page 31). This means that everyone has the right to live in freedom and in safety. But is it really so straightforward?*

FREEDOM

Freedom means different things to different people. For many of us, it means doing what we want, when we want to. Yet there are specific types of freedom, such as being able to practise your religion, or being accepted as an equal by others in your community. This is freedom from prejudice. Being able to say or write what you like is called freedom of speech. Then there is the freedom associated with the right to have a say in how your country is governed. This is political freedom.

⬇ *Specialists uncover human remains in Iraq. These victims of Saddam Hussein's genocidal policies did not live in freedom and safety.*

All airline passengers are routinely searched to comply with airport security.

SECURITY

Security means protection from threats to freedom. These threats can come in many different forms. Crime is a threat to personal freedom, whether it is an attack on ourselves or our possessions. Prejudice, intimidation and injustice are also threats. So is war, and terrorism. We look to our government and our laws to defend us from such attacks on our freedom.

THE RIGHT BALANCE?

Freedom and security are like two sides of the same coin. We cannot consider one without the other. The freedom of a person, or a community, or a country needs protection from those who seek to undermine that freedom, but finding the right balance is not easy.

FACING THE ISSUES

Sometimes, promoting the security of one group of people means undermining the freedom of another group.

In March 2003, the USA, the UK and other coalition forces invaded Iraq. They thought the Iraqi government was developing weapons of mass destruction that might be used against them. Those who opposed the war argued that this was never proved. Some people welcomed the invasion because Iraq's leader, Saddam Hussein, was believed to have been involved in acts of genocide and torture. Others say that the invasion inflicted even more suffering. After the invasion, open elections were held, but many claim that the violence they sparked pushed the country towards civil war. Who is right? And whose rights matter most? It depends on your point of view.

Many Iraqis outside Iraq protested against the invasion. They saw it as a threat to the freedom of Iraq.

ISSUES OF FREEDOM AND SECURITY *have been with us for a long time. From the time of the Ancient Greeks to the present day, rulers, politicians, soldiers and ordinary people have struggled to assert their ideas about how society should operate. Sometimes the balance has tipped in favour of freedom. In times of war it has often tipped back in favour of security.*

The state is shown as a giant in this drawing from Leviathan *by Thomas Hobbes, written in 1651 during the English Civil War.*

THE STATE AND THE INDIVIDUAL

The Ancient Greeks first used the term 'democracy' over 2,500 years ago to describe a society in which men (not women or slaves) were free to have a say in how they were governed. However, most states before the nineteenth century were not democracies – individual freedom was limited by the power of a single ruler. Ordinary people had few rights and were not allowed to challenge the state's authority. Those who protested were often imprisoned, or even executed. Strong government was seen as essential for the stability and security of all.

POWER TO THE PEOPLE

By the end of the seventeenth and early eighteenth centuries, many people in Europe and the USA believed that men should be free to govern themselves. The English Bill of Rights (1689), the American Declaration of Independence (1776), and the French Declaration of the Rights of Man and the Citizen (1789) all proclaimed individual freedom at the expense of interference from the state.

A detail from a painting showing the signing of the US Declaration of Independence, 4 July 1776.

FREEDOM FOR ALL?

However, individual freedom was not available to everyone. The growth of political freedom in the UK, for example, coincided with a rapid growth of wealth and power. This was largely created by the colonisation of other lands to form the British Empire and the slave trade. The British Empire meant economic security for the UK, but a loss of freedom for the countries it occupied, such as India.

THE SECOND WORLD WAR

When a country goes to war, the security of the nation often becomes more important than the freedom of its individual citizens. During the Second World War (1939–45), many governments introduced emergency laws that in peacetime might have seemed unacceptable. However, when invasion threatened, these laws seemed not only necessary, but desirable. Food, clothing and petrol were rationed and everyone had to carry identity papers. The movements of civilians were monitored and many foreigners were rounded up and 'interned' or imprisoned for the duration of the war.

GET THE FACTS STRAIGHT

In times of war, foreign residents and people of foreign descent may be seen as a threat to national security. During the Second World War, almost 120,000 Japanese Americans and resident Japanese people were interned in special camps or relocated to another part of the USA. The UK interned about 8,000 people, mainly Germans and Italians, and Australia interned about 15,000 people, many of whom were sent from overseas.

⬇ *Japanese-American families were relocated after Japan attacked Pearl Harbor, December 1941. The US government was worried that some people may have information that could be used against the USA.*

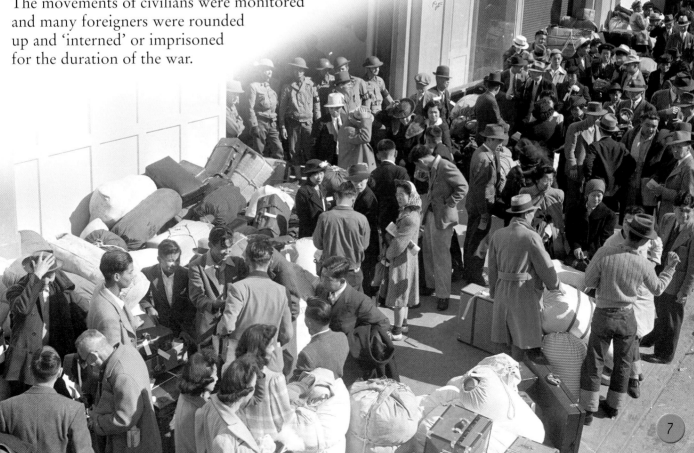

MOST PEOPLE AGREE *that the main job of government is to ensure the freedom and security of all law-abiding citizens. But which is more important – freedom or security? In 1784 US President Benjamin Franklin wrote that 'they who give up essential liberty to obtain a little temporary safety deserve neither liberty nor safety'. Yet in 2006 US President George W Bush told Americans that 'my most important duty is to protect you from harm'.*

ANTI-SOCIAL BEHAVIOUR

Different people want different things from government at different times. In recent years, laws have been introduced in the UK to combat anti-social behaviour, which includes things such as abusive language or drunkenness. Offenders may be given an Anti-Social Behaviour Order, or ASBO, which restricts the places they can go or their behaviour. If offenders breach the terms of their ASBO, they can be sent to prison. However, civil liberties groups complain that young people can be sent to prison for actions, such as swearing, that are not in themselves illegal.

This man is under arrest for drunken behaviour. Most people want to live in a society free from violence.

THE ROLE OF THE POLICE

The role of the police is to enforce the law, protect the public, preserve the peace and prevent crime. But how should they perform this role? Do police powers, such as stop and search patrols or Internet surveillance, bring greater security to the general public? Or do they threaten human rights, such as that of freedom of movement? In January 2006 police in Dubbo, Australia used new powers to 'lock down' a housing estate after clashes with about 100 local residents. The police closed off streets and searched drivers and vehicles. The operation brought the violence to an end, but some people questioned the use of such extreme powers in a residential area.

Police in Australia have the power to stop and search members of the public in certain circumstances. Some people believe this leads to discrimination against minority groups.

FACING THE ISSUES

Sometimes governments have to make extremely difficult decisions about issues of freedom and security. After hijacked passenger planes were deliberately crashed into the World Trade Center in New York in 2001, some governments passed new laws allowing the military to shoot down passenger planes suspected of being hijacked for similar attacks. However, a German court later repealed such a law in Germany on the grounds that the government had no right to kill those on the plane to try and save the lives of others.

IN THE COURTS

The role of the courts is to uphold the laws made by governments. The laws of many countries are based on the principle that a suspect is innocent until proven guilty. In court, such a principle is intended to support the right of the accused to a fair trial. However, some people argue that the rights of the accused should not be more important those of the victim of the crime, or more important than the security of the general public.

SELF-DEFENCE

GOVERNMENTS, THE POLICE and the courts cannot prevent every attack on our freedom and our security. Sometimes, individuals or even whole communities decide they have to protect themselves. Such self-defence may be legal, and accepted by society. However, other types of self-defence are illegal, and are not supported by society. Should people be free to protect themselves in any way they can?

PERSONAL SECURITY

When someone is attacked physically, the laws of most countries allow for the use of 'reasonable force' in self-defence. However, when Cees Gardien shot and killed an armed man during a robbery on his property in Holland in 2003, he was charged with manslaughter. Mr Gardien claimed he had acted in self-defence, but was he protecting himself from armed robbers who might have killed him, or did he use unnecessary violence? A court later found him not guilty of manslaughter but guilty of possessing an illegal weapon.

THE GUN DEBATE

The right of members of the public to own and use guns for self-defence is a controversial issue, particularly in the USA where gun ownership is legal (under certain conditions) and approximately 45 per cent of all households have a firearm. Many people feel that owning a gun gives them protection from criminals or violence. Others argue that guns limit freedom by creating a society in which lethal weapons are accepted.

⬇ *This girl is learning to shoot at a licensed gun club in the USA.*

VIGILANTE GROUPS

People who 'take the law into their own hands' are known as vigilantes. Vigilante groups often form when people feel the government or the police are not protecting them. Some act illegally using violence to deliver their version of 'justice'. Other vigilantes may, for example, trace sex-offenders on the Internet, by illegally hacking into websites and then circulating their personal details. However, not all vigilante groups act outside the law. The Guardian Angels were set up in the 1970s to patrol New York's subways and prevent muggings. They are now an internationally recognised community safety organisation.

FIGHTING BACK?

Self-defence is not always about being aggressive in order to protect ourselves. If you are being bullied, for example, you may feel unable to fight back, but there are many things you can do to help yourself and stop bullying behaviour. You could: tell the bully to go away, tell someone in authority that you trust (such as a teacher), and build up your confidence by attending self-defence classes.

Are these teenagers a threat to passers-by, or should they be free to meet in a public place?

WHAT DO YOU THINK?

People often say they feel threatened by groups of teenagers gathering in residential areas. Abusive behaviour, drugs and shop-lifting all give cause for concern. In 2005, Howard Stapleton from Merthyr, Wales invented a machine that emits a high frequency sound which can only be heard by young people. When his machine, the Mosquito, was installed outside a local store, teenagers quickly moved away, complaining that the noise made them feel sick.

● Do you think that shopkeepers have the right to protect their shops and their customers in such a way?

● Whose freedom matters most – the customers and shopkeepers or the teenagers standing outside?

● Can you think of a better way to sort out the problem?

MANY PEOPLE BELIEVE that the fragile global balance between freedom and security was altered forever on 11 September 2001, when terrorists attacked the USA. Since then, governments have sought to protect people from similar attacks by waging what is known as 'the war on terror'.

⬆ The two bombs that exploded at a tourist resort on the island of Bali in 2002 killed 202 people and injured many more, mainly Indonesians and Australians. A terrorist group with links to Al-Qaeda claimed responsibility.

ACTS OF TERROR

Terrorists seek to provoke fear by carrying out violent attacks against civilians in order to achieve political, religious or ideological aims. The terrorists who carried out the attacks in the USA belonged to Al-Qaeda, a group of Islamic extremists who have sworn to fight a 'holy war' against those who oppose them.

Al-Qaeda is not the only terrorist group. Groups in Spain, Northern Ireland, Peru, the Middle East and Sri Lanka have all committed acts of terrorism, often in the name of 'freedom' or 'liberation'. However, Al-Qaeda are considered the greatest threat by the international community, because their campaign is worldwide. They are suspected of involvement in terrorist attacks such as the Bali bombings in 2002, the Madrid bombings in 2004 and the London bombings in 2005.

NEW LAWS

After the attacks of 11 September 2001, many governments passed new anti-terror legislation. For example, in the USA the government now has less restricted access to telephone and Internet records. In Australia, people can be held under a new offence of 'association with terrorist groups'. Civil liberties groups argue that many of these laws threaten our freedom, such as freedom of speech. However, other new laws such as tighter border controls have been passed without serious opposition.

INTERNMENT WITHOUT TRIAL

Many laws are based on the principle that anyone accused of a crime is innocent until proven guilty. However, recent acts of terrorism have caused some governments to reconsider this principle. Should someone who is acting suspiciously near an airport, be arrested and held without trial? Such action may result in the imprisonment of innocent people, or it may prevent a terrorist attack.

GET THE FACTS STRAIGHT

- The Patriot Act (see page 30) was passed in the USA on 26 October 2001, six weeks after the terrorist attacks in New York.
- According to a Gallup poll in January 2002, 47 per cent of Americans wanted their government to stop terrorism even if it reduced their civil liberties.
- A later Gallup poll in February 2004 revealed that 71 per cent disapproved of one provision of the Patriot Act, which allows government agents to secretly search a US citizen's home without telling them.

GUANTANAMO BAY

In October 2001, the USA and its allies invaded Afghanistan to destroy Al-Qaeda. Captured suspects were sent to a US military base at Guantanamo Bay, Cuba. Many of these suspects, of different nationalities, are still being held without trial – for indefinite periods. In 2006, the UN condemned this as a breach of human rights. However, the USA argued that the detainees were not prisoners of war, but 'illegal combatants', who do not require protection under US law.

⬇ Detainees at Camp X-ray, Guantanamo Bay. The people in orange are terrorist suspects who are being held without trial.

IDENTITY CARDS

CAN YOU PROVE YOUR IDENTITY? *Do you want to? Passports, driving licences and credit cards are all forms of identification. They carry personal information and give us access to travel and services. But what about a card that everyone has to carry? Can compulsory identity cards protect us against fraud, smuggling and terrorism? Or might they limit our freedom?*

 Some cards have an electronic chip that holds information unique to the owner, such as fingerprints or an iris scan. This is known as biometric data.

GET THE FACTS STRAIGHT

Different countries have different approaches to ID cards:

- USA – no ID card. Driving licences are widely used for this purpose.
- UK – considering ID cards with iris scans, fingerprints, and other biometric data to be held on a national database.
- Germany – compulsory ID cards carry a wide range of information and are protected by some of the strongest privacy laws in the world.
- Australia – rejected a national ID card scheme in 1987. Some politicians want to reconsider it.
  - Holland – police can stop and fine anyone aged 14 years old or over for failing to carry some form of official identification, such as a passport, driving licence or ID card.

EXISTING CARDS

Many countries already have compulsory identity cards, including Brazil, Belgium, Israel, Spain, Germany and Malaysia. These cards include personal details such as name, address, age and a photograph, and may also carry information such as blood group, country of birth or fingerprints. In countries where there is no compulsory ID card, people may be asked to produce a passport or driving licence as proof of identity.

A temporary shrine to the victims of the Madrid bombings in 2004. Compulsory ID cards in Spain did not prevent the bombings because the terrorists did not try to hide their identities.

NEW PROPOSALS

Mohamed Atta, one of the men who carried out the terrorist attacks of 11 September 2001, used several fake identities. After the attacks, the UK government wanted to introduce a national identity card that would, in the words of one government minister, prevent the UK becoming 'a soft touch for terrorists'. However, the aims of the proposed card were not just to improve national security. The government also emphasised their usefulness in preventing fraud, detecting crime and enforcing immigration controls.

Opponents of ID cards argue that documents, such as passports, already provide a secure means of identity.

SECURING OUR IDENTITIES

Those in favour of ID cards say that they protect our freedom by ensuring that criminals and terrorists cannot steal our identities and use them to commit crimes. They argue that those with nothing to hide should not fear ID cards, as personal details will not be shared without good reason. Forgery can be avoided by the use of new technology, such as iris scans and digital fingerprinting.

LIMITING OUR FREEDOM?

Opponents of ID cards worry that the information ID cards contain will be shared amongst different government agencies, threatening our privacy. If ID cards are compulsory, what powers will the police and the courts have?

BIG BROTHER?

IDENTITY CARDS *are not the only way to keep track of people. Schools, employers, tax and benefit offices keep records about us. Information about what we are doing is stored every time we log on to our computers or walk past a CCTV camera. Most countries have laws to prevent this information getting into the wrong hands. But is enough being done to safeguard our privacy?*

➡ *This is a sequence of pictures from CCTV cameras showing suspects on bicycles wanted in connection with a murder. Most town centres are now watched over by CCTV.*

NEW TECHNOLOGY

Collecting information about people is not a new issue. However, new technology has allowed more types of data to be collected, stored and shared than ever before. Telephone and Internet companies log our calls, credit card companies monitor shopping habits, and biometric data is being introduced into some passports. Criminals may have their DNA recorded on a database, and their movements may be monitored by electronic tags. Most of these measures are designed to protect us, but civil liberties campaigners think they erode some of our basic freedom.

PRIVACY LAWS

Some countries have privacy laws to protect people from the misuse of personal information, such as selling email addresses to businesses looking for new customers. But in the battle against terrorism and serious crime, the police and other law enforcement agencies want more powers to examine private financial records, stored text messages and emails. They argue that new laws are needed because of the way people now communicate. Journalists, on the other hand, fear that new laws may force them to reveal the identities of anonymous informers.

⬇ *Tagged criminals are released from prison but have their movements recorded.*

↑ *A small CCTV camera on a bus. Is CCTV an invasion of privacy or does it help you feel safe?*

UNDER SURVEILLANCE

Every law-abiding citizen wants to feel safe from criminals, and most of us have become used to CCTV cameras in shopping centres and bag searches at airports. But some people are becoming more concerned about new methods of surveillance that search randomly for suspicious behaviour. One such method is the introduction of Automatic Number Plate Recognition on UK motorways. The police argue that this will help them track and catch criminals. Civil liberties groups want to know why the police need details of every car journey every innocent driver makes.

WHAT DO YOU THINK?

Governments often say that those of us with nothing to hide have nothing to fear from surveillance and data collection. Groups such as the International Campaign Against Mass Surveillance, say that our governments seek nothing less than the collective monitoring of entire populations for the purposes of social control. What do you think? Does more security always lead to a loss of personal freedom?

FREE SPEECH

FREE SPEECH MEANS BEING ABLE

to say or publish what we like. Most countries regard this as a basic human right. Any restriction on free speech is known as censorship. Yet not everyone sees free speech as a 'good' thing. What if it offends people? What if it provokes unrest, violence or extremism?

⬇ *During a political conference in Boston, USA, US security officials set up an enclosed 'free speech zone' or FPZ – caged pens where people are allowed to demonstrate. This woman has gagged herself to protest against the use of FPZs because they contradict the principle of free speech.*

A DEMOCRATIC RIGHT?

The French philosopher Voltaire (1694–1778) once wrote 'I disagree with what you have to say, but I shall defend, to the death, your right to say it.' For many democratic countries, free speech is essential. Without it, voters would not know about different political parties and elections would not be free and fair. Threats to free speech are often met with fierce opposition from the public. Yet free speech also means that people are free to say untrue things, and express offensive opinions.

Pens Are For ANIMALS!

FREE SPEE THE 2ND VICTIM OF 9-11

A THREAT TO SOCIETY?

In reality, most countries have laws restricting free speech to some degree. Libel laws, for example, make it illegal to print deliberate lies about someone. Certain opinions are deemed so offensive or dangerous to society that they are banned from public expression. In Austria, it is a crime to deny the Holocaust, when millions of Jews and others were slaughtered during the Second World War. Nevertheless, a British historian, David Irving, did just that and in 2006 he was sentenced to three years in prison. Some people are now calling for this law to be changed.

THE LAW OF INCITEMENT

After the terrorist attacks of 11 September 2001, many governments became concerned that future terrorists might be encouraged by the speeches and writings of Islamic extremists. When Abu Hamza, a Muslim cleric, was jailed in the UK in 2006, the judge said 'you are entitled to your views and in this country you are entitled to express them, but only up to the point where you incite murder or use language calculated to incite race hatred. That is what you did.' Nevertheless, some people fear that the offence of 'incitement to religious or racial hatred' may restrict freedom to criticise religion, or make jokes about it.

*Peace and blessings be upon Him

FACING THE ISSUES

In September 2005, a Danish newspaper published cartoons of the Prophet Muhammad*, the last of the Prophets of Islam. Several of these cartoons depicted him as a terrorist. Muslims around the world objected strongly, as any image of the Prophet Muhammad* is considered an offence against Islam. Many non-Muslims, however, argued that banning the cartoons amounted to censorship. Other newspapers had to decide whether to reproduce the cartoons or not. If they did, were they responsible for stirring up hatred between Muslims and non-Muslims? Or was freedom of speech worth defending, at any cost?

⬅ *Protesters in Karachi, Pakistan burn the Danish flag in protest after the publication of cartoons of the Prophet Muhammad*.*

GOVERNMENT SUPPRESSION

Not all countries uphold free speech. Some regimes actively suppress it to silence opposition and maintain control. According to human rights organisations, Myanmar (Burma) has one of the world's most repressive regimes in which there is no freedom of speech; mail is intercepted, telephone conversations are monitored and fax machines and computers are banned.

WHEN WE LOG ON to the Internet, chat online and check emails, we enter an electronic world of seemingly endless possibility. Facts, fiction, gossip, news and information can be accessed instantly, at the click of a mouse button. But should the Internet be a free and unregulated resource, or does it need to be limited and controlled?

ACCESSIBILITY

The Internet is a worldwide system of computer networks carrying information and services. Anyone can create a web page, post an opinion, spread news and, potentially, say or read anything they like without outside interference. In most countries access is not regulated, or censored. For many people the Internet is a modern day guardian of free speech.

⊕ *Billions of emails are sent and received every day, but do we know where they have come from and who wrote them?*

GET THE FACTS STRAIGHT

Online chat rooms enable children to speak freely to each other, as equals. But how safe are they?

● In one Canadian study, 43 per cent of children who use chat rooms said they had met someone on the Internet who asked for personal information about them, such as an address or telephone number.

● A US study, meanwhile, revealed that 12 per cent of 8–18 year olds had discovered that someone they were communicating with online was an adult pretending to be much younger.

● STAY SAFE! When online, stay in public areas, never give out personal details, never open an attachment unless you know and trust the person who sent it, and never agree to meet someone without telling your parents and taking a responsible adult with you.

ANONYMITY

Internet users can access services anonymously, using different names or codes. This protects those who fear they may be persecuted for their views. But it also protects terrorists, smugglers and paedophiles, who increasingly use the Internet to plan and carry out their crimes. As a result, in some places such as Australia, governments have introduced laws to enable police to access Internet records. Yet it is not just the police who are increasingly able to access information from our computers.

SECURITY

Many people use the Internet to process highly sensitive information, such as credit card details. Much of this information can be encrypted, or coded, to stop criminals accessing it and stealing money or an identity. However, some criminals, known as 'hackers', can still break into supposedly secure Internet sites. Other criminals use techniques such as 'phishing', where emails are sent to people asking for their bank details, or 'spyware' programmes which enable someone to access personal files. Many of us rely on software, such as a 'firewall', to protect us from breaches of personal security. Privacy and data protection laws make it difficult for the police to stop security breaches completely.

CENSORSHIP

The communist government in China exercises strict censorship of certain anti-government material. In 2006 it signed a deal with Internet company *Google* to set up a search engine, but with access blocked to thousands of 'sensitive' websites. *Google* responded to criticisms of this self-censorship by arguing that limited access to its services was better than no access. However, critics argued that *Google*'s decision merely encouraged state censorship.

⬇ *Protesters in Dharmsala, India were angry after* Google *announced a censored version of its search engine for use in China. The Chinese government has strict censorship laws.*

POLICE STATE?

WHEN A GOVERNMENT uses force, intimidation or other tactics such as secret surveillance against the general public, it is often labelled a 'police state'. However, 'police state' can mean several different things. Is it where the laws themselves are repressive, or is it where force and intimidation are applied against the rule of law?

➜ *Brian Haw is the only person allowed to demonstrate inside the Houses of Parliament security zone. He was there before new anti-terror laws were approved, but if he leaves he cannot return.*

⬆ *Riot police in France confront a group of protesters. Governments can introduce emergency measures to control people.*

FIGHTING TERROR

Many people believe that better policing will help to make our communities secure. But how do we feel when police powers are directed against ordinary citizens? Anti-terror laws in the UK, for example, have given the police greater powers to stop and search members of the public, to arrest, fingerprint and photograph suspects, and to detain those involved in peaceful protests within one kilometre of the Houses of Parliament. Prime Minister Tony Blair said of these new laws 'we are not living in a police state but we are living in a country that faces a real and serious threat of terrorism'.

EMERGENCY POWERS

In October 2005, riots flared up in inner-city areas across France. Many of the rioters were young men from ethnic Arab and African minorities, who said they felt discriminated against. Thousands of vehicles were set alight and people ransacked schools and churches. The government responded by declaring a state of emergency, allowing it to bring in thousands of additional police officers and establish curfews.

No government describes itself as a 'police state', but critics may use the term to mean any of the following:

- The use of torture in interrogation
- Broad police powers to stop and detain members of the public
- The use of the police or military for political ends
- Rule by fear and intimidation
- Use of 'emergency powers'
- The use of secret surveillance
- Government censorship.

TOTALITARIAN REGIMES

Regimes that come to power through force, or rule without free and fair elections, often use the police or the army to control the population and crush opposition. After fiercely contested elections in Zimbabwe in 2005, President Mugabe launched 'Operation Clear Out the Trash', in which tens of thousands of people in poor townships were arrested by armed police or had property confiscated and destroyed. President Mugabe said the operation was to protect Zimbabweans from disease and criminals. Opposition groups, however, believe the motive was to punish those who voted against him in the elections.

⬆ *Police in Harare, Zimbabwe look on as houses in a township are demolished.*

BORDERS

ACCORDING TO THE UN, all law-abiding people have the right to leave any country, including their own, and to return to their country. Yet in practice, freedom of movement across borders is not so straightforward. War, political and cultural differences, economic threats and crime mean that states prevent unrestricted access for reasons of security.

BORDER CONTROLS

Border controls include documents such as passports and visas, as well as physical barriers such as fences and the security personnel who patrol them. Many countries have tightened their border controls since recent terrorist attacks, making it more difficult for people to gain entry.

IMMIGRANTS

Terrorism is not the only reason for border controls. Governments also seek to 'protect' their citizens from unrestricted immigration. An immigrant is someone who chooses to live in a different country, usually for work. They may bring valuable skills and encourage economic wealth. Or they may put a burden on the existing population, competing for jobs and services. Illegal immigrants are those who remain in a country without permission. They often work in low-paid jobs where they are less likely to be detected.

◀ *A US border patrol officer watches the border between the USA and Mexico. Of the estimated 10-12 million illegal immigrants in the USA, about 75 per cent are believed to cross the border from Mexico.*

Asylum seekers are people who attempt to stay in a different country because of fear of persecution in their own country. In recent years, some countries such as the UK have faced growing numbers of asylum seekers from war-torn countries such as the Congo and Afghanistan. The UK government detains and deports anyone whose claim for asylum cannot be verified.

● Should the government offer a 'safe haven' for those who have been persecuted elsewhere?

● Or should it be made even more difficult for those claiming asylum to cross national borders?

THE EUROPEAN COMMUNITY

The European Union, or EU, consists of 25 member states, with others set to join in the coming years. One of its main purposes is to establish free movement between member states across internal borders. More freedom for citizens of the EU generally means tighter controls along its external borders. However, some people are concerned that recent enlargement has exposed the EU to a new wave of internal immigration from poorer member states. They believe that a large-scale movement of people could threaten the cultural and economic balance of wealthier EU countries. Such issues of freedom or security have at times threatened to overwhelm the European Parliament.

⊘ *Illegal immigrants tunnel under a fence at the Eurostar terminal in Calais, France. They are hoping to get to the UK by stowing away on a train.*

PR 28

MILITARY OCCUPATION

MILITARY OCCUPATIONS HAVE been happening for centuries. One country invades another and uses its armed forces to establish control over the resident population. In the past, countries have invaded each other to seize assets or gain more territory. Nowadays, with international laws in place to deter such aggression, military occupiers are more likely to justify invasion on the grounds of safeguarding national security.

ALLIED OCCUPATION

At the end of the Second World War, Allied forces occupied Germany. The four occupying powers – France, the UK, the USA and the Soviet Union, divided the country into four zones of control. The four zones were treated differently, according to the aims and wishes of their occupiers. At first, Germany was treated harshly, but then the USA and UK in particular saw that it was in their interests to revitalise the German economy. They could profit from helping to rebuild the country and from trading with a new democratic government.

⬆ *An Israeli soldier talks to a Palestinian at a checkpoint between Jerusalem and Ramallah, a modern-day disputed territory.*

DISPUTED TERRITORY

In 1948, the UN declared the creation of a Jewish state – Israel – from land that had belonged to Palestine. Since then, conflict between Israelis and Palestinians has centred on a number of disputed territories. One Palestinian area, known as the Gaza Strip, was occupied by Israeli forces until 2005. When troops withdrew, Israel maintained exclusive control of airspace over the area and made military incursions across the border. The conflict, and efforts to resolve it, continue to focus on issues of security and the right of both sides to exist as a free and sovereign state.

INVASION OF IRAQ

When the US-led coalition invaded Iraq in 2003, it became an occupying force. Many people both inside and outside Iraq protested that the occupation was illegal. Others argued that coalition forces had a responsibility to stay until the fighting died down and the new government was secure.

FACING THE ISSUES

Other disputed occupations include:
- Morocco's occupation of Western Sahara
- Israel's occupation of the West Bank
- China's occupation of Tibet.

All locations are seen by their occupiers as strategically important areas, vital for security as well as culturally significant. However, many people of Western Sahara, the West Bank and Tibet seek independence in order to assert their political freedom and cultural identity.

Coalition troops in Iraq deliver aid to the civilian population.

THE WORLD TODAY CONTINUES to struggle with issues of freedom and security. We seek protection from the threats of crime, war and terrorism, yet we also fear what we do not know. Different religions, different politics, different national interests create tensions that quickly escalate. So what can the international community do to redress the balance?

UN negotiators are called in to resolve disputes in some countries in an attempt to prevent armed conflict.

THE ROLE OF THE UN

The UN was set up in 1945 with the aim of preventing war by promoting a common need for security. It tries to settle disputes without violence, and member states contribute towards an international peace-keeping force. One of its most successful interventions was in East Timor, where an Australian-led force oversaw the withdrawal of Indonesian troops in 1999. However, the ability of the UN to act depends on the agreement of its member states. As a result it has been accused of failing to intervene in some crises, such as the genocide in Rwanda in 1994.

THE ARMS RACE

Countries that feel threatened often seek to protect themselves by stockpiling weapons or maintaining large armies. This in turn may be seen as a threat by neighbouring countries, and an arms race begins. In the 1990s, rivals Pakistan and India both tested nuclear bombs. Most states have now signed international arms control treaties.

President Pervez Musharraf of Pakistan (centre, left) poses with officials at the test site of a nuclear-capable missile in March 2005.

FREEDOM FROM FEAR?

In January 2005, Condoleeza Rice, US Secretary of State, said 'if a person cannot walk into the middle of the town square and express his or her views without fear of arrest, imprisonment or physical harm, then that person is living in a fear society, not a free society. We cannot rest until every person living in a 'fear society' has finally won their freedom.' But did this mean that the US might actively intervene in those countries such as Zimbabwe, Iran and Myanmar that she identified as 'outposts of tyranny?' The governments of those countries protested that the USA had no right to impose its views.

WHAT DO YOU THINK?

In many ways, cooperation between different nations of the world has never been greater. Peace is negotiated, international treaties are signed and ideas, goods and people are exchanged with great ease. Yet still the world is not safe. Our different ideas about freedom and security come from our different perspectives – Arab or Jew, East or West, radical or moderate. These ideas aren't just for governments to debate, they affect everyone, even everyday people just walking down the street.

Do you think your country has achieved the right balance between freedom and security?

GLOSSARY

Automatic Number Plate Recognition: A new camera system that can identify car number plates. It can be used to monitor the movement of cars for security reasons. The data is stored on a computer.

biometric data: Information based on human physical traits. It includes iris scans, fingerprints and facial images.

CCTV: (Closed Circuit Television) A network of cameras that sends images to operators who use them for security purposes.

censorship: Stopping something being said or shown.

civil liberties: Protection from government power and the safeguarding of human rights such as freedom of speech. Civil liberties groups campaign to preserve these rights.

colonisation: The gradual occupation and control of countries by people from another country.

curfew: An order to stay inside at set times.

democracy: A type of government in which the leaders are elected by the votes of the general population.

DNA: The building blocks of every living thing. Every person's DNA is unique.

extremism: When somebody holds extreme views. Often they take drastic action to achieve their aims.

fraud: Criminally deceiving someone in order to gain from them, usually financially.

genocide: Purposely killing people from an ethnic group in order to wipe them out.

human rights: The basic types of freedom that everyone should have (see page 31).

ideological: Something that relates to the collected ideas of a group of people; their ideology.

incitement: When somebody is encouraged to do something that is wrong.

internment: The act of holding someone against their will, usually during wartime.

intimidation: When someone is frightened and forced to do something they do not want to.

legal system: A way of creating and enforcing laws in a country. It includes the courts and the police force.

libel: When something untrue is published about someone.

liberty: another word for freedom.

paedophiles: Adults who are sexually attracted to children.

Patriot Act: This new part of US law was introduced after the attacks of September 2001. It gives greater powers to the US security services at home and abroad.

prejudice: When someone forms an opinion without considering all the facts, for example, racial prejudice.

rationed: when the amount of something a person can have is controlled. Food and other goods were rationed during the Second World War so that supplies did not run out.

surveillance: When something or someone is watched closely.

totalitarian: A system of government that seeks to control every aspect of people's lives, often by force or intimidation.

weapons of mass destruction: These include any weapons that can cause death on a massive scale, such as nuclear and chemical weapons.

FURTHER INFORMATION

United Nations (UN)
This site provides information on the work of the United Nations as well as the complete text of the Universal Declaration of Human Rights.
www.un.org/rights

Liberty
The website for one of the UK's leading campaign groups for free speech and civil liberties.
www.liberty-human-rights.org.uk

Gateway to the European Union
A multi-language portal to information about rights, policies, borders and security issues within the European Union.
www.europa.eu.int

Australian Government Attorney-General's Department
Click on 'National Security' and then 'Legislation' for a summary of current anti-terror laws in Australia.
www.ag.gov.au

The White House
Includes a summary of the US National Security Strategy and official views of the 'war on terror'.
www.whitehouse.gov/infocus/nationalsecurity/index.html

Crime Reduction
Gives examples of different kinds of anti-social behaviour and the legal options for dealing with it.
www.crimereduction.gov.uk/asbos9.htm

Safekids
A useful and comprehensive guide to safety issues concerning children and young people on the Internet.
www.safekids.com

UK Identity and Passport Service
A government site explaining new UK proposals for identity cards and the problems associated with identity theft.
www.identitycards.gov.uk/index.asp

Amnesty International
Website of the international organisation working to protect human rights worldwide, featuring campaign news and up-to-date reports.
www.amnesty.org

Every effort has been made by the Publisher to ensure that these websites contain no inappropriate or offensive material. However, because of the nature of the Internet, it is impossible to guarantee that the contents of these sites will not be altered. We strongly advise that Internet access is supervised by a responsible adul

UNIVERSAL DECLARATION OF HUMAN RIGHTS

On 10 December 1948 the General Assembly of the United Nations adopted the Universal Declaration of Human Rights. The rights it proclaimed were intended as a universal standard for all peoples and countries of the world. They include:

- The right to life, liberty and security of person – everyone should be allowed to live in freedom and in safety
- The right to freedom of movement – everyone should be able to travel freely, leave their home country and return to their home country
- The right to freedom from torture – no one should be treated cruelly or inhumanely
- The right to equality before the law – everyone should be treated fairly by the police and the courts
- The right to a nationality – no one can have their nationality taken away
- The right to freedom of thought, conscience and religion – no one should be punished for their beliefs.

For more on human rights, go to the UN website listed left.

INDEX